AF605671

THE CORAL REEF BOOK

CHARLES HOPE

There are more animals and plants living on coral reefs than any other ecosystem. They support thousands of species of coral, fish, plants and many other animals.

Coral reefs are hugely productive ecosystems. About a quarter of all marine species depend on them for food.

Coral reefs are both strong and fragile. They have been around for millions of years, yet they can be easily destroyed. Natural and human-made problems, such as coral bleaching, are a major threat to their survival.

Corals are living organisms made up of tiny animals called polyps. Lots of identical polyps join together to form a colony.

Corals are invertebrates, just like their close relative the jellyfish. Invertebrates are animals that do not have a backbone.

Corals are related to sea anemones. Both of these animals have tentacles that they use to capture prey.

Coral reefs thrive in warm, tropical oceans, in clear water and close to the surface. This is because most corals need sunlight to survive.

Coral reefs need sunlight because of the symbiotic relationship between corals and zooxanthellae. These are a special type of organism called dinoflagellates, and they can live inside the tissue of coral polyps.

In return for shelter and a closer position to sunlight, zooxanthellae provide energy to their coral host. They do this by making nutrients from sunlight by a process called photosynthesis. Zooxanthellae are responsible for up to 90 per cent of the energy that corals need to live.

Zooxanthellae, along with pigments inside the coral itself, give corals their brilliant colour.

Aside from zooxanthellae, corals can get nutrients by eating marine organisms called plankton. These are tiny life forms found in the water.

Different types of plankton include squid, worms, algae and fish.

Corals reproduce sexually. This is when sperm and egg cells are joined together. Corals do this by releasing their eggs and sperm into the water.

When coral egg and sperm cells combine

Coral larvae attach themselves to rocks or other hard surfaces and begin to grow.

Waves and ocean currents spread egg and sperm cells to a wider area, encouraging coral growth. They also help by transporting food to the corals.

There are three main types of coral reef: fringing reefs, barrier reefs and atolls. The most common are fringing reefs, like this one, which can take up to 10,000 years to form.

Fringing reefs have two main parts. The first is the reef flat, which is closer to land and the water's surface

The reef slope is further
away from land and in deeper

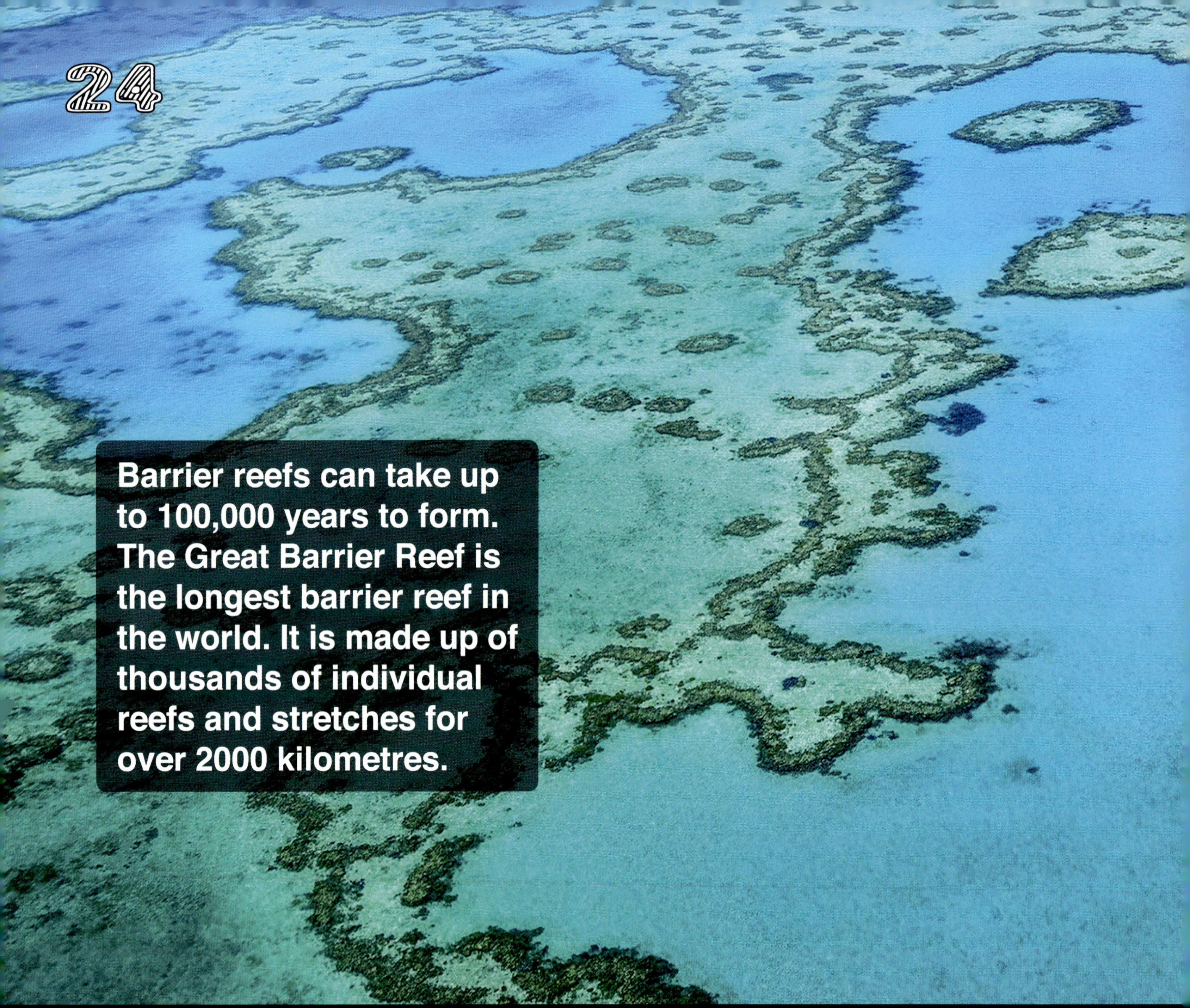

Barrier reefs can take up to 100,000 years to form. The Great Barrier Reef is the longest barrier reef in the world. It is made up of thousands of individual reefs and stretches for over 2000 kilometres.

Barrier reefs grow parallel to the shore, and are separated from land by a deep channel or lagoon

Barrier reefs help to
protect coastlines from

An atoll is a circle-shaped coral reef surrounding a lagoon. They can take as long as 30 million years to form.

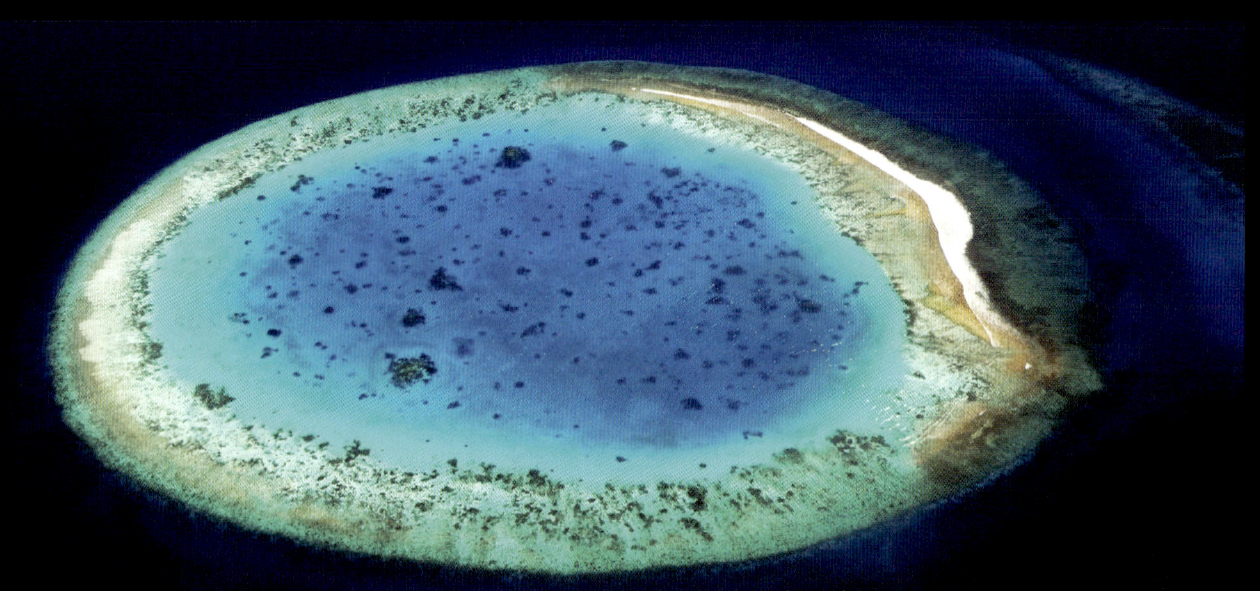

Over millions of years, the island that once formed the centre of the atoll may submerge into the ocean, leaving behind a lagoon.

An atoll may have an island surrounded by a lagoon and coral reef. These atolls are popular as holiday resorts for tourists.

Cays are small sandy islands found on the surface of coral reefs. They are formed by ocean currents moving and depositing the remains of plants and animals that lived in the surrounding reefs.

Soil and plants may appear on cays, making it possible for humans to live on them.

There are over 2000 species of coral. Hard corals, such as staghorns, have a tough skeleton made of limestone.

Table corals benefit from being flat as they receive more sunlight, which helps the zooxanthellae inside the coral make energy

Pillar corals can grow several metres tall. This gives them an advantage when reefs are crowded

Soft corals, like this tree coral, do not have a tough skeleton. This means they can move from side to side with the ocean currents.

Gorgonians, which are known as sea fans because of their shape, are tall, wide and thin.

Bubble corals remain inflated during the day, and deflate when it becomes dark.

Coral reefs are home to many different types of marine animal. This includes Christmas tree worms, which make their home by burrowing into coral skeletons.

Flamingo tongue snails attach themselves to sea fan corals, which they like to eat.

Nudibranches are related to snails, though they do not have a shell.

Many different types of crustacean live in coral reefs. Candy crabs like to eat soft corals, and often stick bits of coral on their shell to use as camouflage.

Jellyfish have existed for over 500 million years, despite not having a brain. Many species are found in coral reefs.

Starfish have varied diets. Some like to eat snails and algae, while others eat rotting waste.

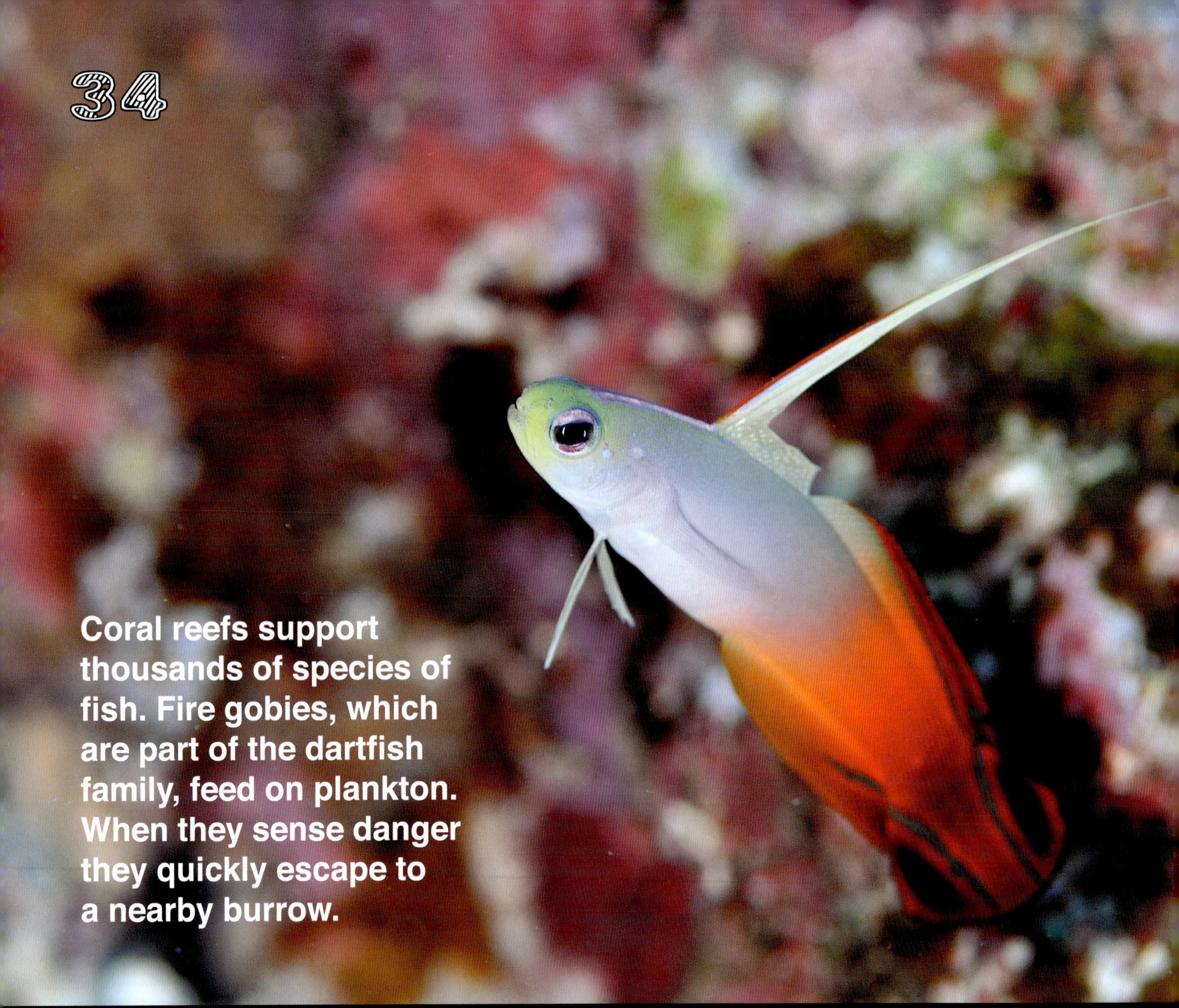

Coral reefs support thousands of species of fish. Fire gobies, which are part of the dartfish family, feed on plankton. When they sense danger they quickly escape to a nearby burrow.

Most surgeonfish, like the blue tang, feed on algae found in coral reefs, which helps to maintain the overall health of the ecosystem.

Lionfish are dangerous predators that hunt many types of fish in coral reefs.

Some animals only spend a small amount of time around coral reefs. This is often the case for larger animals like dolphins.

Several species of sea turtle use coral reefs as feeding grounds. They eat sponges, seagrass, corals, jellyfish, shrimps and algae.

Manta rays visit coral reefs to stay clean and healthy.

Like all ecosystems, coral reefs are home to deadly predators. Gray reef sharks are excellent hunters with a strong sense of smell. They like to eat fish, squid, octopus and crustaceans.

Banded sea kraits are venomous sea snakes. They spend time on land and in the ocean, and eat eels and small fish.

Great barracudas are one of the top coral reef predators. They eat a variety of fish, squid, octopuses and shrimps.

Even some of the smaller animals that live in coral reefs are dangerous. Stonefish are the most venomous fish in the world.

Blue-ringed octopuses are one of the most venomous animals on Earth. The rings only become blue when they feel threatened.

Cone snails hunt small fish and marine worms with their venomous harpoon. They can be very dangerous to humans.

Symbiosis plays an important role in coral reefs. This is when different organisms interact with each other in a beneficial way. One type of symbiosis is commensalism. This is when one organism benefits without having any impact on the other.

Imperial shrimps use sea cucumbers for transport. This helps them to save energy while helping and cover a wider area when looking for food.

An example of commensalism is when a crab uses coral as a hiding place from predators.

Decorator crabs stick bits of their coral reef environment all over their body, which helps camouflage them from predators.

Mutualism is a type of symbiosis that benefits both organisms. Corals and zooxanthellae have a mutualistic relationship. Corals provide the zooxanthellae with shelter, while the zooxanthellae provide nutrients to their coral host.

Clownfish and sea anemones benefit from mutualism. The fish receive protection, while the anemones receive food drawn to it by the fish.

Boxer crabs carry anemones in their claws to shake at predators. The crabs receive protection, while the anemones receive scrap food left over from the crabs, which are messy eaters.

A common form of mutualism takes place at cleaning stations. These are special locations on reefs where smaller animals gather to eat the parasites and algae found on larger animals that come and visit.

Turtles regularly visit cleaning stations so that surgeon fish and other animals can clean the algae from their shell.

Cleaning stations benefit both groups of animal. The smaller animals are fed, while the larger animals are kept clean and healthy.

Manta rays, which grow up to seven metres wide, take advantage of butterflyfish, which like to eat the parasites they find on larger fish.

The cleaner shrimp is commonly found at cleaning stations.

Cleaner shrimps will even enter the mouths of visiting animals, such as moray eels, when looking for food

Some visiting animals, such as groupers, can change colour. This signals the shrimp to approach and makes the parasites easy to see

The bluestreak cleaner wrasse is also a hard worker at cleaning stations.

Cleaner wrasse eat parasites wherever they find them, even from the eye of this oriental sweetlip.

Dangerous animals like this pufferfish pose no threat when they visit cleaning stations, allowing the cleaner wrasse to work in peace.

Coral reefs are under threat from a wide range of natural causes. Some marine animals, such as the foureye butterflyfish, eat corals as part of their diet.

Members of the parrotfish family eat corals.

Crown-of-thorns starfish eat large amounts of coral polyps in Australian waters.

Some reefs are harmed because they are exposed to hot and cold temperatures during low tide.

Corals exposed to the air may suffer from wind damage.

When exposed during the day corals can overheat and dry out, and expel the zooxanthellae they need to survive.

Violent weather can quickly destroy large areas of coral reef.

The destructive power of cyclones and the waves they create can kill entire reefs.

Coral reefs are under threat from a variety of human-made problems. The fishing practice of bottom trawling is similar to a bulldozer driving through the corals.

Carelessly placed fishing nets damage and destroy corals.

Overfishing affects the food chain that coral reefs depend on for survival.

Coral reefs are popular tourist attractions for scuba divers. Many divers are unaware that corals can be damaged by touching them.

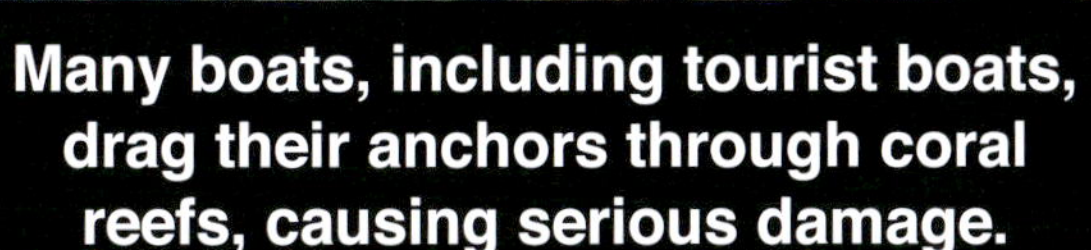

Many boats, including tourist boats, drag their anchors through coral reefs, causing serious damage.

Some tourists do not realise that corals can be killed by walking on them.

Pollution is extremely harmful to coral reefs and other marine life. Sewage, rubbish, chemicals and oil spills all poison the fragile ecosystem and limit the amount of sunlight that reaches the corals.

In some parts of the world, sewage flows directly into the ocean

Water pollution can lead to coral diseases and harmful algae. These algae can deprive coral reefs of the sunlight they need to grow

Many people use beaches as rubbish dumping grounds. This rubbish often finds its way into the water.

Waste products that enter the ocean can leach chemicals into the water that harm corals and other animals.

Sedimentation is when large amounts of sediment – such as sand, plant remains, rocks and minerals – are carried by rivers into the ocean. This harms coral reefs because it reduces the amount of sunlight they receive, and chokes the corals.

Land erosion greatly contributes to sedimentation. This may happen when land is cleared of vegetation for farming.

Logging increases erosion and the amount of sediment that ends up in rivers.

Mining causes a larger amount of sediment in rivers.

Mangrove forests, which act as a natural filter of river sediments, are being harvested to make way for farmland.

In recent years Earth has became warmer. Many of the factors that contributed to this were the result of human activity. 'Global warming' has caused ocean temperatures to increase around the world, sea levels to rise and the number of cyclones to grow. This has affected the health of coral reefs everywhere.

Most corals can survive in water between 20-28 degrees Celsius. When water temperatures become too warm, corals respond by pushing the zooxanthellae out of their tissue, and eventually die. This turns the coral white and is known as bleaching.

Artificial reefs are built from old ships, concrete blocks and other human-made objects, and allow corals to attach to the hard surfaces.

These artificial ecosystems encourage corals to grow, and help to attract and support other marine animals.

Coral reefs are valuable ecosystems that need our protection. There are many ways you can help them to survive.

Recycling: reduces the amount of pollution made by humans.

Planting trees: means less sediment reaches the ocean, and helps to reverse the effects of global warming.

Conserving water: reduces the amount of harmful sewage and pollution that enters the ocean.

Rubbish disposal: litter that is not properly thrown away can find its way into the ocean.

GLOSSARY

ALGAE a type of marine plant.

ARTIFICIAL something made by humans; does not occur naturally.

BURROW to dig into something.

CAMOUFLAGE the natural colouring of an animal that helps it blend into its environment.

COLONY a group of plants or animals living together.

COMPLEX something that has many different and connected parts.

CONSERVE use less of; save.

CRUSTACEANS a group of invertebrates found mostly in the ocean, and which usually have a hard covering.

DEFLATE let air or gas out.

DIVERSE lots of different things.

ECOSYSTEM a community of living things and the environment where they live.

EROSION when soil is taken away by wind or water.

EXCREMENT waste materials that come out of an animal.

EXPEL force out.

HABITAT the natural environment of an animal.

HARPOON sharp spear.

INFLATE fill with air or gas.

LAGOON body of salt water separated from the sea by a coral reef.

LARVA an early stage of a creature's life.

LOGGING cutting down trees.

MARINE found in the sea.

NEMATOCYST a type of stinging cell found in the tentacles of coral polyps and jellyfish.

GLOSSARY

NUTRIENT a substances that helps living things to survive.

ORGANISM a living thing.

PARALLEL two lines that are side by side, with equal distance between them for their length.

PARASITE an organism that lives in or on another organism, and at their host's expense.

PHOTOSYNTHESIS a process used by some plants and organisms where sunlight is used to make nutrients.

PIGMENT the natural colouring matter of animal or plant tissue.

POISON a substance that can cause injury or death to a living thing.

POLLUTION Harmful chemicals in air, water or land.

POLYP a tiny individual organism that makes up corals.

PREDATOR an animal that kills and eats other animals for food.

PREY an animal that is hunted and killed by another animal for food.

PRODUCTIVE makes a lot.

REEF a ridge, or strip, of coral.

SEWAGE waste water and excrement.

SPECIES A group of animals that live and breed together in the wild.

SYMBIOSIS the interaction between two different organisms, involving benefit to one or both organisms.

TENTACLE a thin limb on an animal, usually near the mouth.

VEGETATION plants.

VENOM a substance that can cause injury or death to a living thing.

ZOOXANTHELLAE tiny organisms living in the tissue of many corals.

First published in 2016 by
wild dog
54A Alexandra Parade
Clifton Hill Vic 3068
Australia
+61 3 9419 9406
dog@wdog.com.au
wdog.com.au

Printed and bound in China by 1010 Printing International

National Library of Australia
Cataloguing-in-Publication data:
Creator: Hope, Charles, 1981.
Title: The Coral Reef Book.
ISBN: 9781742034140 (pbk)
Target Audience: For primary school age.
Subjects: Reef ecology--Juvenile literature,
Coral reef ecology--Juvenile literature.
Dewey Number: 577.789

Wild Dog would like to thank Dr Renata Ferrari (Spatial & Quantitative Ecology Postdoctoral Fellow, The University of Sydney) for her careful fact checking, and Neil Conning for his thorough proofreading.

10 9 8 7 6 5 4 3 2 1 16 17 18 19 20

Front cover: Clownfish
Title page: Denise's pygmy seahorse
Imprint page: Tiger tail seahorse
Back cover: Loggerhead sea turtle

PHOTO CREDITS:
Images courtesy of Shutterstock and Wikimedia Commons.
Front Cover Lotus 41; p 1 timsimages; pp 2-3 Brian Kinney; pp 4-5 Vlad61; pp 6-7 Ethan Daniels; pp 8-9 Steven Fish; p 8 dibrova; p 9 In Depth Solutions; pp 10-11 Designua; pp 12-13 soft_light; pp 14-15 Andrey_Kuzmin; pp 16-17 Tyler Fox; p 18 borzywoj; p 19 Napat; pp 20-21 Rich Carey; p 20 Narrissa Spies; p 21 Kirill Umrikhin; pp 22-23 Tanya Puntti; p 22 Ethan Daniels; p 23 Ethan Daniels; pp 24-25 ProDesign studio; p 24 Ignatius Tan; p 25 Pete Niesen; pp 26-27 sashahaltam; p 26 VVO; p 27 ArtTomCat; p 28 tororo reaction; p 29 AustralianCamera; p 30 (main) Ethan Daniels; p 30 (bottom left) Ethan Daniels; p 30 (bottom right) John A. Anderson; p 31 (main) Rich Carey; p 31 (bottom left) serg_dibrova; p 31 (bottom right) Pete Niesen; p 32 (main) JonMilnes; p 32 (bottom left) Vilainecrevette; p 32 (bottom right) YUSRAN ABDUL RAHMAN; p 33 (main) reezuan; p 33 (bottom left) Vlad61; p 33 (bottom right) fenkieandreas; p 34 (main) divedog; p 34 (bottom left) divedog; p 34 (bottom right) John_ Walker; p 35 (main) alekss-sp; p 35 (bottom left) Krzysztof Odziomek; p 35 (bottom right) Ethan Daniels; p 36 (main) Pete Niesen; p 36 (bottom left) Rich Carey; p 36 (bottom right) Shane Gross; p 37 (main) Sorapong T; p 37 (bottom left) Paranee Hansakul; p 37 (bottom right) LauraD; pp 38-39 Jung Hsuan; p 38 LauraD; p 39 Ekkapan Poddamrong8; pp 40-41 Marius Meyer; p 40 Richard Whitcombe; p 41 Jung Hsuan; pp 42-43 Matt Haeger; p 42 Durden Images; p 43 Fiona Ayerst; p 44 (main) antos777; p 44 (bottom left) alain pardon; p 44 (bottom right) Dan Exton; p 45 (main) Levent Konuk; p 45 (bottom left) Boris Pamikov; p 45 (bottom right) Hans Gert Broeder; p 46 (main) Pete Niesen; p 46 (bottom left) simak; p 46 (bottom right) Ethan Daniels; p 47 (main) BeeBright; p 47 (bottom left) Stephen Gibson; p 47 (bottom right) Ethan Daniels; pp 48-49 irabel8; p 48 pio3; p 49 Ethan Daniels; p 50 (main) muratart; p 50 (bottom left) Rich Carey; p 50 (bottom right) Strahil Dimitrov; p 51 (main) Dudarev Mikhail; p 51 (bottom left) Mumemories; p 51 (bottom right) Chad Zuber; pp 52-53 Tigergallery; p 52 (bottom left) hans engbers; p 52 (bottom right) Richard Whitcombe; p 53 (bottom left) Fabien Monteil; p 53 (bottom right) Richard Whitcombe; pp 54-55 Dr. Morley Read; p 54 (bottom left) B Brown; p 54 (bottom right) TFoxFoto; p 55 (bottom left) Kamzara; p 55 (bottom right) Ethan Daniels; p 56 Dudarev Mikhail; p 57 Ethan Daniels; pp 58-59 aquapix; pp 60-61 Andrey_Kuzmin; p 60 (bottom left) Phovoir; p 60 (bottom right) g-stockstudio; p 61 (bottom left) Monkey Business Images; p 61 (bottom right) Maciej Bledowski; p 64 Ekkapan Poddamrong8; Back Cover Willyam Bradberry.

FSC® is a non-profit international organisation established to promote the responsible management of the world's forests.

Charles grew up near Wagga Wagga, a country town far away from the ocean. Given that open water terrified him, he was happy where he was.

It took many years for Charles to realise the ocean was full of wonderful things. Scuba diving on school camps opened his eyes to the world beneath the waves, and he hasn't looked back since. Though if he ever sees a shark up close, he will make like a squid and ink his way out of there.

Charles is an editor, proofreader, picture researcher and freelance writer.